the true keeps calm biding its story

Winner of the 2008 James Laughlin Award

of the Academy of American Poets

The James Laughlin Award is given to commend and support a poet's second book. It is the only second-book award for poetry in the United States. Offered since 1954, the award was endowed in 1995 by a gift to the Academy from the Drue Heinz Trust. It is named for the poet and publisher James Laughlin, who founded New Directions Publishing Corp.

Judges for 2008:   Rae Armantrout   Claudia Rankine   Bruce Smith

Winner of the Sawtooth Poetry Prize 2007

Peter Gizzi, judge

the true keeps calm biding its story

Rusty Morrison

 AHSAHTA PRESS

Boise State University • Boise • Idaho • 2008

Ahsahta Press, Boise State University
Boise, Idaho 83725
http://ahsahtapress.boisestate.edu

Printed in the United States of America
Cover design by Quemadura
Book design by Janet Holmes
First printing January 2008
ISBN-13: 978-0-916272-98-2

Library of Congress Cataloging-in-Publication Data

Morrison, Rusty.
    The true keeps calm biding its story / Rusty Morrison.
        p. cm.
    "Winner of the Sawtooth Poetry Prize 2007"—T.p. verso.
    ISBN 978-0-916272-98-2 (pbk. : alk. paper)
    I. Title.

PS3613.O7777T78 2008
811'.6--DC22
                            2007026321

ACKNOWLEDGMENTS

My thanks to the following publications, where some of these poems first appeared: *Barrow Street:* "not simply to lie on grass . . . "; *Boston Review:* "sky speaks . . . ," "with practice . . . "; *Coconut:* "it was once believed . . . ," "my pleasures inventoried . . . ," "pale fingers . . ." ; *Columbia Poetry Review:* "sullenly disposed . . . ," "the petals of poppies," "to set the table as if . . . "; *Eleven Eleven:* "a gnat . . . ," "how to hold what remains . . . ," "the hill's grasses . . . ," "walked barefoot . . . "; *The Modern Review:* "breadcrumbs . . . ," "here I place . . . ," "I might travel his death . . . ," "just long enough . . . ," "the coat-rack's narrow . . . ," "there are thoughts . . . "; *Parthenon West:* "like water spiders . . . ," "just lean against the wallpaper . . . ," "the chainlink . . . "; *Pleiades:* "an aimlessness . . . ," "my stammering mind . . . ," ; *Verse:* "a breeze . . . ," "elaborately frilled edge . . . ," "fill a page . . . ," "for months after his death . . . ," "here again is the counting of linoleum . . . ," "my new skin . . . ," "shaded but not rested . . . ," "silently my father's dying . . . ," "the vertebrae achieved . . . ," "though my first foray . . . ," "today a ringing-in-the-ears . . ."; *Volt:* "the sun setting . . . ."

I'd like to thank the poets who gave me their wise counsel and their insights about poems that are now a part of this manuscript: Julie Carr, Robin Caton, Patricia Dienstfrey, Grace Grafton, Alice Jones, Andrew Joron, and Melissa Kwasny.

I am very grateful to all the teachers who have read my poems and given me their critical and creative guidance—whether in workshops during my first years of college, or during my return to grad school later in life, or in private sessions outside of academic institutions: Chana Bloch, Joshua Clover, Susan Griffin, Lyn Hejinian, Brenda Hillman, Diana O'Heir, Elizabeth Robinson, and Richard Silberg.

I am honored and very grateful that Peter Gizzi selected these poems.

This work was selected by Susan Howe as the winner of the 2007 Poetry Society of America's Alice Fay Di Castagnola Award for a manuscript in progress.

for Ken

our finitude as human beings

is encompassed by the infinity of language

—Hans-Georg Gadamer

The border makes up the homeland. It prohibits and

gives passage in the same stroke.

—Hélène Cixous

Contents

nine

one

please advise stop

pale fingers of inheritance do not disintegrate until they touch us stop

meaning collapses on the inhale please

gestures too quick to catch are the guarantors of the given stop

the true keeps calm biding its story stop

the arsonist's perspiration stains the sky black please

the gray-and-white patched cat licks her paw till value becomes again incalculable stop

I wasn't traveling westward only into the power of its place-names stop

the water puddle sways like an earthbound kite stop

the stickiness of this instance seals within it every expression of its menace please advise

please advise stop

sky speaks with an accent like worship stop

a temporary lifelessness in your eyes where I pour my waiting palaces stop

the pearliest part of a memory is lost to its lack of consequence please

rub a little chalk on both palms and then reach stop

was I the mad girl eyes white like blossoms stop

or just the rescuer who turned accomplice please

so cold the air is granular against skin's gray stop

I bang this thin sheet of tin and call it listening stop

do the reckless simply hear the avalanche before the rest of us please advise

please advise stop

my pleasures inventoried like cutlery stop

no histrionics just two brass lamps a stack of old newsprint from Paris tied in twine stop

the glamour is in asking first *Are you happy?* stop

I'm elongating the upward curve of my handwritten "f" please

years of growth sanded away to make this beautifully varnished myth please

the stories so often describe the homecoming as some kind of relief stop

the flower stems will always seem to break at the water line stop

locked in the grandly tapestried room while upstairs the phone rings stop

touch the velvet gone stiff from fingers' sweat please advise

please advise stop

the hill's grasses are lavender in conversation with evening light stop

how to narrate my lateral glance without fastening stop

a balancing of emotions would require fewer objects free-floating please

slip my hand in to earth neither tearing nor imploring but touring at the speed of loamy
roots stop

balancing could be cross-blending without overlapping please

when I'm attentive as if to a lecture how little will green have revealed stop

in my sympathies a prickly contagion stop

how to touch sky with fingers cool as windowpanes stop

this desire for cohesion of ends to beginnings so guileful an enemy please advise

please advise stop

a breeze can't re-ascend its sublime escalator stop

oscillate but don't gadfly between out- and in-wardness stop

mics as well as headphones hidden in a field of wildflowers please

how to have repentance without squeezing the memories from it stop

a perfect topographic recall in the mind of a just opening bud stop

with the greatest care a green adjusts to my gauge of its distance please

struck moodily the fallen trunk touching not even the extremity of my relation to the
vegetal stop

pleats of forgiveness accordion but never entirely unfold stop

prideful and unqualified when I chance into the pollen room please advise

please advise stop

walked barefoot in the spill of loamy earth between redwoods stop

accompanied by no sermon stop

my repetitive gesture will eventually wear through its surrounding world please

I heard a drawer pull open but not its philosophies rearing up in jagged peaks stop

how to walk off the hackles we raise so carelessly stop

how does a sequence continue to startle its way through clouds of conclusions please

wash one's face of any resemblances before they mingle stop

I don't see color in the window at moonrise but feel it a dampness on my forehead stop

tattooed both wrists with the holy idea but only skin deep please advise two

please advise stop

I was dragging a ladder slowly over stones stop

it was only from out of my thoughts that I could climb stop

not from the room please

my father's dying offered an indelicate washing of my perception stop

the way the centers of some syllables scrub away all other sound stop

his corpse merely preparing to speak its new name at the speed of nightfalling please

each loss grows from a previously unremarkable vestigial organ stop

will I act now as if with a new limb stop

a phantom limb of the familial please advise

please advise stop

only gray rocks with drifting mist but I was so in need of something paired stop

each pairing isolates another world stop

attempted listening in a lower register than I usually speak please

still snapped inside the brackets of my old maneuver but not blindfolded by it stop

teeth grinding down their desperate impulses stop

shine the thought's dark mahogany until it begins to shift like a shoal of mackerel please

soon will I be able to discern the linen texture of right silences stop

there have been emphatic emissaries stop

a pebble cupped in a rose-petal held by a palm resting on the lawn please advise

please advise stop

basin of hills polished with the pour of sunset please

easing down on one knee to touch the oak leaf trapped in a footprint stop

I neglect then compromise the vision I've hidden between eye movements stop

cup my palms together for something new to grow in their microclimate stop

spit as if intending to hit what you aim at stop

a skirtful of fresh pears rolling onto the lawn and into the stealth of narrative please

how to line the pockets of madness with flowerpetals please

the months go but my father's death stays demanding to be reabsorbed stop

sylph-like grass misty rain conceived against claims of other empires please advise

please advise stop

the chainlink fence holds separate the severed air stop

a blond boy sits on a bench his hair dissolving into wind please

etch kohl around each shadow to give it room rather than brightness stop

look up into a starless patch of night and watch it expand stop

stand in its corridor as if in motion stop

as if all four directions had let go of their point of interlocked origin please

indices that at once augment and ridicule the senses stop

a stone floor to step into waist deep stop

too easily I might erect in lieu of sight a stage of sculpted shrines please advise

please advise stop

like water-spiders on a pond the hours pass overhead stop

with each perfected dexterity I thin the surface that carries me stop

traces of an otherwise indiscernible consensus collect under my fingernails please

his face isn't lost to me but traveling now and mostly untended stop

hereafter will I apply rules and avoid content stop

braid wildflower stems peeled of petals stop

scrub gently with a brush to relieve us of the historical present please

listen for the entire circumference of the screen door's arc but hear only its slap stop

even incoherent babbling is usually phonetically accurate please advise

please advise stop

any object inclines away from memory the more energetically I imagine its features stop

featureless is the vault in which I want to hide myself undetected stop

haven't I even a pigeon's sense to fly suddenly the other way please

pecking at seeds and not the shadows of seeds among the gravel stop

we say *materialized out of nothing* to further secure the brackets of that rigid frame stop

a magnet linked tight to other magnets can still pull in new metal stop

impossible to lift the weightless gravity of nightfall please

staring into the dark like digging a grave through an already existing grave stop

tonight Cassiopeia the Pleiades are emitted from the sky like fragrance please advise

three

please advise stop

with practice a memory like a voice can be thrown into any unsuspecting object stop

each thought is a cone that depends on its opening at both ends stop

I need a few ants to appreciate the sugar-white of bed sheets stop

unfolding the paper crane won't undo its allegiance to sequence stop

the features emanating from clouds are more fierce through an open window stop

each breath's devotion to transparency fails to convert my flesh stop

I mark my room with all five of my senses but soon it is strange again stop

the intoxicating smugness of a black felt hat's softness stop

pinholes pressed through paper fill immediately with shadow please advise

please advise stop

just lean against the wallpaper its flower-pattern flares stop

tied up my dry bundle of consciousness with fresh twine stop

how to wait out the empty frame gold-leafed and needing polish stop

scrubbed away the furniture until I was left with only the housekeeping stop

the frown thinning my lips went unnoticed by the rest of my face please

close to form today but didn't penetrate more than formula stop

knock do not rub the earth from freshly collected potatoes please

midday sun through the window-slats and fitted to the wall like a handrail stop

even numbness has downy tufts and pods that split to release seeds please advise

please advise stop

nearness is a funnel into which I keep pouring my loneliness stop

each vow of truthfulness is darkly overhung with a rampart of prophecy stop

the visible is overtaking and undertaking me at the same time please

my fingerprints smile back at me shyly stop

please after please visiting the statue for a cure stop

chance my madonna of melting snow please

to finish a pain once it starts is my intimate companion stop

those who were insulted drank more on the average than those who were not stop

the woman I suspect of philosophy is swollen with an alien light please advise

please advise stop

the vertebrae achieved their balance individually and wouldn't reconcile stop

lie down in wet grass and be caulked please

ashes from the dying fire form a last calibration of the updraft stop

how to measure my meaning with lamps not clocks please

the scavenger picks a bit of prudence from his teeth and spits stop

the aspen burned down to aftermath and no further stop

sun is whitening the sum of summer grasses without adding them up stop

dried and stuck on a pin is today's insect of my inattention stop

willow branches sweeping the air of damage please advise

please advise stop

my stammering mind isn't quick enough at its wardrobe changes stop

the tendon in silence drawn tight through every room of the house stop

turned on the heater then off again then on please

a single oak beam at the apex of the peaked ceiling directs time's flow stop

in the dark follow any smoothness clean as straw stop

on my nightstand an empty glass is not self-canceling stop

all the furniture of observation needing to be stacked away like folding chairs stop

I practice opening my cursive circles to let through more sunlight stop

guilt is still my first form of fastening please advise

please advise stop

shaded but not rested under the rickety arbor I make of consciousness stop

any edge can be sharpened to rip right through sky's cellophane stop

some toxins ornament at first please

lizard fixed to a stone as if it were the stone's lung stop

emotion is derived from the Latin *exmovere* meaning *to move out of or away from* stop

the banister offers its stability even as it flees up its flight of stairs please

was I shoring up my safety on the wrong side of the embattlement stop

pine knots on a varnished plank aren't weaknesses but stored-up personality stop

the ragged scar frilled the edge of the kitten's ear please advise

four

please advise stop

just long enough to dry my eyes and not to want to reopen them stop

an instinctive blindness with its prow going so quick in the current stop

to inhabit an absence takes great balance stop

two banks of a river as if a choice were always offered stop

but the flowing comes from only one mouth please

the long inhale of a cigarette the short exhale of a sunset stop

moth by moth measuring each night's hiatus stop

hiding the given in the guise of distance stop

the dark is thin tonight a blue vein showing its pulse please advise

please advise stop

here again is the counting of linoleum tiles in place of remembering stop

the accumulation of stains on a surface becomes a site of burials stop

each particle of my nature has its own past stop

clouds today various as minerals displayed in a glass case stop

despite their fragility each relic preserves me stop

all is consignment until I am healed of my selectivity please

the quiet presses like a palmful of gravel against my cheek stop

a sudden wind against my forehead has forever changed my shape stop

a breach of regulations a cubbyhole left empty in the table of elements please advise

please advise stop

breadcrumbs were really the ones swallowing birds stop

opened the door but not the depth of attention that my entry demanded stop

pressed spiders between a book's pages cure holiness stop

traveled the circumference I could learn from it the center stop

a stain spreads under table linen and avoids being caught stop

. not the idea but behind it a patron saint with green eyes please

the blind priest's eyes were wide as a countertop and white as washed parsnips please

the stone in my pocket need only be called a globe stop

stripped of its leaves and branches the sky is all the more hidden please advise

please advise stop

a pleasure to rub the rough grout between smooth tiles stop

some household objects tilt forward to separate from darkness stop

a red lacquered bobby pin holds firmly a few wispy strands of memory please

when I was young thought entered me easily as the aroma of steeping cassoulet stop

a silt on the surface of any piety that's left too long unstirred please

what fingers tapping on a prayer-book will do to the prayer stop

I recite reasons as if they were saints' names stop

every afterward is afflicted with the past's companionship stop

still sucking jam from the cool lip of the jam-jar solemn and down on both knees
please advise

please advise stop

my new skin craves the scratch of dead leaves stop

retrieve comes from *re-* plus *trover* meaning not only *to find* but also *to invent* stop

fingers will intuitively test the patches where cognizance is thinnest stop

receive without asking kindness to look under its mask stop

to move dramatically without embarrassment I emptied my stage of performers stop

can a memory ever admit it no longer recognizes itself please

even the most adaptive concentric circles cannot link as a chain stop

we fasten no more loyally than drops of water in a rainspout stop

and as fundamentally please advise

please advise stop

I saw the window spread its wings a white heron stop

each feather a corridor into the many-storied structure drawing itself skyward stop

the further its remove the more distinct the opening of each pinion stop

just as the past sees more exactingly than this instant in its temporal imprisonment stop

just as looking up through an oak's openwork dome is a kind of falling stop

nothing in the room need foreshorten into perspective stop

not distractions with their complicated nests of stolen fabric stop

not the beating of wings but one wash of the wing my head wrenched back stop

nothing that simply appeases will ever mean vision again to me please advise

five

please advise stop

I might travel his death a creaking and swaying beneath me stop

there are static expressions freed now and passing along the walls stop

an object isn't what is hidden but what smiles out from the hiding please

with only the slightest effort I might abandon every father stop

or read them all cover to cover please

eyes turn like the telling of stories first inward then out stop

the next page wasn't the kind of listening I wanted but it was all I was offered stop

to reveal as in the Latin *re-* plus *velum* meaning *veil* stop

the thought of him still everywhere only a new place to hide please advise

please advise stop

my father's dying makes stairs of every line of text seeming neither to go up or down stop

that I make the nodding motion to help myself feel I understand stop

in common with his bafflement I find comprehension alone will not suffice stop

that I begin to find other books in other rooms were always the same book stop

affiliation which comes from the Latin *ad-* plus *filius* meaning *son* stop

a correct word would steady more than itself like a banister please

first will I need to write any one of the letters that neither of us wrote to the other stop

one cannot predict but only open the hands that are inherited stop

and watch what they do please advise

please advise stop

there are no words on the wall of daylight where night abandons me stop

no words but letter after letter inky and staining stop

outlines are the limit of each letter which otherwise might reach out to infinity stop

always some missing pages in the book I am reading a second time stop

in time even the most insisting objects are ruefully done away with stop

within the instances of my father's dying I was merely passing along the walls stop

peeling off strips of wallpaper because I have abandoned other languages stop

will I ever stop trying to hide the books in the meanings I gave them stop

or my father moving swiftly ahead of reason and outside word's reach please advise

please advise stop

here I place *father* as if the word could mend itself stop

up into the corner of the room only one corner of the room and silently stop

just to stay pressed in that corner with no one looking up to see stop

a falling I am frightened of what he couldn't say he was watching stop

the spilling gesture of a swallow's body before its wings again pick up wind please

the living entities a viewer makes of everything in the viewing field please

as if I could take them up and that would mean become them stop

all the needful ways to position myself conspicuously at his side stop

rather than the patience of bed and table and window in his last room please advise

please advise stop

there are thoughts he must have entered though they were only half-open stop

my father who entered but then there was what only a death could leave stop

as I watched stop

portions of that past adhere to what my thinking pales and floats away from me stop

portents that I imagine to make my thinking hard and tangible please

I place a figure in a window vaguely lit a father in a room stop

a predatory imagination will stalk every difference it discovers stop

even shapelessness is itself a separate thing but faltering I stare it down to fact stop

only air can measure itself against whatever it finds please advise

please advise stop

sieved the stillness until it produced a fine dust stop

cleaned the ashtrays of absolution down to a blessing stop

the gambler rubs his tongue over his front teeth reading them like cards please

as the startled pigeons rise together their unity could hold water stop

each leaf cat-faced and purring shine stop

if I'd listened to myself as each unconscious emphasis fluttered its pennant stop

laconic aphids on the rose bush iconic green flies on the porch rail stop

the quiet in the air tonight will create each landing before it descends stop

how am I to reappear from nowhere without practice or premeditation please advise

six

please advise stop

the driver wasn't guilt-wracked but a pedestrian who saw the accident lost her sense of
smell stop

according to the gondolier each wave strikes the hull in a different language stop

I find a new direction because every planet stays locked in its orbit stop

no way to tell the weeds that are flesh-colored from the flesh that is weed-colored please

listening is a composite of glossing novelty and following my fears around in the dark stop

emptied of questions and filled instead with the night-sky's hooded throng stop

the road to the asylum forks each time I genuflect please

the entire morning gone callow with a rationale stop

now even the least leaf rustling must be theatricalized please advise

please advise stop

a gnat flying as if leaning back to catch a late-blossoming in the breeze stop

no center inside the creaturely where I might carve a keeping place stop

gift candy left in its tin since a perfect reciprocity was achieved without eating it please

pretending to keep up the conversation a white handkerchief followed a flock of geese
into the pond and drowned please

a huge walled-off deity affixed at the edge of my outer life stop

formed composure not a discrepancy between raucous flowering vetch and a few pale
daisies please

if the story was not intended for me why was I holding my breath stop

I found the door open but couldn't take my eyes from the small locked blue window stop

tiny cloud-white drops caught leering out from the skeleton of branches please advise

please advise stop

I add brush-strokes to my visions to thicken their surface courage stop

novelty prodding me with its impatience-stick stop

my flashlight held high under the blanket stop

we can't let the actual contain us the same way every time stop

the sound of a rolling boil is satisfying and frightening stop

it's the past that's finishing every sentence for me please

between the sigh and the laugh was it a genuine repair or a quick dab of polish stop

the low ceiling was uncoiling at the exact speed I recoiled from it stop

grant the visible its pronouns and watch it disappear please advise

please advise stop

though my first foray to the palm reader will be tantalizing stop

the patterns of linoleum squares never meet but the floor goes on endlessly stop

the door slightly ajar measures me please

broken glass litters the street with a kind of loneliness that might precede a growth
spurt stop

I think I hear nature repeat but it merely stares back at me please

face of a passerby acts as an astringent and the past seals up again stop

all the chances are stalking the audience not the protagonist please

will I die still the kneeling woman dressed in wool stop

always another horse in the high meadow damp fetters and chest heaving please advise

please advise stop

it was once believed that metals grew in the earth the way plants fill air stop

skin of my fingertips pulling itself taut to receive sensation stop

this stubbly chapped rough-cloth is my passion and nostalgia stop

erecting my window to hidden faces and wrapped hands please

touch this last flash of sunset where it cracks the glass city stop

I turn into the mineral of my obsessive imagining please

floodlit in an otherwise lost memory please

an inner harbor where mice scuttle from ship to docked ship stop

the chord sung must be higher because I've gone to roof's edge to sing it please advise

please advise stop

sun setting so quickly away from us and never the proper calibration to our instruments stop

orchestra of my attachments excessively over-rehearsed stop

in the echo of warped floorboards I needn't concoct a further predicament please

technicians may already be waiting for me in a small future fiercely equipped for such
purposes stop

why should exoneration belong to only one of us searching out the eyes of the other stop

I hear your knees begin to buckle as you perform your ancestors' ardencies stop

behold flesh as the moving center of a functional harmony please

night might still be floating somewhere above us its blood supple and aromatic stop

the swamp frogs sound to us only our own fugitive affections please advise seven

please advise stop

an aimlessness I can't quiet down to inactivity stop

quail's call because to say *lament* would be thick with self-reference please

stammered out the sentence till it completely surrounded the singular clarity stop

spackle of a cloud-pattern falls point-for-point across magnolia blossoms stop

rub consonance until it sparks please

walk as though every step carries with it the edge of earth stop

raindrops creaturely in their crawl across the mosaic plaque stop

an unexpected foreshortening of perception is also called revelation stop

my sudden disorientation echoing as if ancestral please advise

please advise stop

attempting again proximity with the dead as though they stay in place unmoved stop

as though I could measure closeness if I scratched it with tiny marks stop

opened again the fine pleating that opening each time damages stop

as if it were a stranger's hand my hand again replaying the reaching out it failed to do stop

gauging the weight of each inherited object ignoring the object itself stop

dwelling increasingly on the floor between memory and involuntarily pushing memory
away stop

a few darknesses are inward a few are outward pointing branches in a stand of poplars stop

reason can't bring over something on the verge of real but unwilling to become it stop

I can paint any blue on a ceiling and none on the sky please advise

please advise stop

there was no moment of his death to see until it had already passed stop

now looking means drawing a line around each thing daring it to cross stop

I keep my palms clean for this and dry stop

like leaves in wind even the thinnest actions rake over me only to disappear stop

left with color and shape as meaning's only custodians stop

warily I turn my face not sure my eyes will follow please

the humming bird I've caught in a cotton towel will vanish if the towel is opened stop

the cellar I dig will store the hungers not the rations stop

how to tell what must be kept and what must be kept provisional please advise

please advise stop

silently my father's dying attends to the details of his disappearance stop

no cut-glass chimes in fierce wind stop

no furtive closing of a door stop

a silence that is audible and without message stop

a silence from which I am excluded can teach me only exclusion's precision stop

there is a motion in his death like a microscope lens focusing stop

as though everything outside my eyes' and ears' dominion turns to watch stop

a precision into which I can pour whatever I want to believe stop

becomes an oblivion please advise

please advise stop

wind is winter's reflection among the branches stop

true likenesses are never planned stop

though magnifications may be choreographed please

sky falls through every window differently stop

irresistibly drawn into a sudden intake of breath is the thought that fits its shape please

ocean's water absorbed into air is severed from its predictive tides stop

only as the season changes will I see which fears are migratory stop

which of the empty voices have erected for themselves limestone walls stop

into the dark trees invite the darker birds please advise

please advise stop

the petals of poppies orange the eye with after-color stop

elm leaves more hidden by other leaves aren't dark but rather more deeply lit stop

how to hear the wind without developing an immunity please

evening comes without infringing on daylight's shadow stop

completely intelligible until I try to repeat within myself each silhouette please

bear the moments becoming only flecks of black in my kitchen's gray linoleum stop

inevitability but not infinity in the sidewalk's repetition of pavement squares stop

my palms itch as if the skin were cheap fabric stop

all the between in the story leaving itself un-captioned please advise

eight

please advise stop

sullenly disposed to needing the sound of a second no stop

rootless in jars geranium-cuttings already telling time stop

spidery cracks in the wall's plaster the breath of coarse masonry beneath stop

with each invasion of new furniture the same parade music please

patches of original carpet-color shine like exposed modesty stop

an impatience stiff and aromatic as sticks of cinnamon stop

crows on the lawn their shine so black it staunches modification please

some skies must remain unrecognizable to be kept stop

in the dark my flashlight is eager to toss its tight-fisted gleam please advise

please advise stop

the coat-rack's narrow arms rise up empty and flourishing stop

the quiet pulls an empty swing until it seems to move stop

keep one hand free to feel for the parts suddenly lost and moving away stop

the spoonful of honey goes on grinding its bees stop

brush away the interviewing but keep the intervening light please

the day beveled with chaos ripening routine stop

each wild iris invested with the exact countermovement of my observation stop

the mistranslation thick with clocks ticking an inaudible patience stop

again took up the begging bowl of self-explanation please advise

please advise stop

tasted a weedy stain under the robin's song stop

scavenged the cloud-cover with an erect posture stop

fog leaching a gold nimbus from the fresh-mown lawn stop

string the white beads on black cord stop

promise each outline significance not inevitability please

degrees of fortune and misfortune merge as moonlight across the bed stop

within the costume of aphorism a thought flees extinction stop

in the commonplace are curled the whorl of unreadable tracks stop

around the evaporating error remains an indelible after-hue please advise

please advise stop

the rustle of a Sunday bundle of newspapers tucked under my father's arm stop

and no father walking toward me stop

on the branch only oak leaves reddening as wind ripens their talent for exodus stop

on the lawn a scatter of wrens head-down but tail-erect stop

no bringing back the other world though every silence sounds for it stop

soft hiss then only all the rattle of useless memory caught in the unwieldy bundle of his dying stop

where I've tied it stop

waiting for the proscenium that the warblers' song might once again build around me stop

I purse my lips in an exaggerated exorcism of breath please advise

please advise stop

fill a page with words never letting a single phrase form stop

not for avoiding but for allowing what refuses to be remembered stop

displace all practiced confessions with a small shudder stop

I sit long enough to feel the vines along my cerebral canopy entwine please

in the quiet concussions of an unintentional sigh please

steam rising from my soup as if simmering had applied to it the pentecostal stop

cold springtime the climate I assign to surround each church bell's tolling stop

twelve-tone glow of lake water in starlight stop

kept imagination busy testing its talismans please advise

please advise stop

to set the table as if fastening back together fault-lines stop

the folds in my map taking precedence over roads please

the shortness of the hour suggests the ease with which it gained power over me stop

frightening to find abandoned dockyards boarded-up flophouses in my most careful
designs stop

thick gather of lilac petals hand-crushed until scent is a way-mark please

accidentally tipped the weightless exchange that makes sleep simple again stop

the favored color dryly scrutinizes its latest backdrop stop

a rain-soaked newspaper on the porch exuding steam stop

the seized revelation suddenly meek and lapping milk please advise

nine

please advise stop

I throw a stone into air as if every motion were his motion come back to me stop

will is its own endless distraction stop

how many kinds of sight have I condensed into blindness stop

institute a side and there's no end to drawing a longer and longer disturbance line stop

too singular the father I have thinned to a divining stick stop

so many sticks and stones strewn beside the gravel that grinds and gives under my feet please

my every demand for direction already raided of its corporeal continence stop

microscopic organisms are absorbed in every breath but none are penetrable stop

always there will be a past and no need of ingenuous retrieval please advise

please advise stop

not simply to lie on grass but to finesse from the fine blades a rescue stop

scraped surface but not deep enough to enter its changing maze please

in every difference a muffled babble never predictable or predictive stop

more fragile concealments merely group around a new emphasis for cover stop

low wind through oaks and rowans too easily translates as long and short stop

counting is more a stance than an observation please

a stance very smooth and waxen but wherever weakened there are underlights stop

fingertips worrying right through their cotton gloves stop

tonight I again attempt moonlight as though it were a question please advise

please advise stop

elaborately frilled edge of endive enacts a fragile steerage through day's heat stop

the most succulent curtains are immensity's camouflage stop

in the strict sense no apparition runs counter to appearances please

between the blackberries a frothy mold protective as styrofoam stop

to bind means *compel* as well as *unify* stop

how to step out of my watchfulness the thickness of its second skin please

here is the orderliness in genetic logic its wall of curtained windows stop

wind in the winter jasmine will undulate but not accumulate stop

to demand is to already have instituted a ruined world please advise

please advise stop

how to hold what remains but not refine it stop

the door will only open if the structure begins to lean stop

a dark blue satin scrap rubbed between two fingers prizing and vexing stop

let me mortalize and not try to appease the skin when it is cold or still please

afterwards is achievement if it subsumes all apologies stop

a room only seems blind because of the speed with which all its surfaces see me stop

in the humic concentrate of backyard soil feel bodies in their orbits stop

observing my hands as they disappear stop

scent of eucalyptus impassable road in even the mildest winters please advise

please advise stop

for months after his death I adopted deafness stop

I was unexpected but otherwise innocuous in the flock of gulls flying out to sea stop

but couldn't obliterate all of dying's instruments playing discordantly stop

a prickly soreness in staring at everything too long stop

saw the bright band of light between floor and curtain hem but not what dissolved stop

lost buttons and broken cups I tried to treat as mediators please

suddenly-recalled grief in the centers of suffocatingly red flowers stop

held the unearthly glide of a pearl necklace just above my flesh stop

certain insomnias must be shaped into adornment please advise

please advise stop

today a ringing-in-the-ears quality in breathing stop

landscape gave a brief account of itself then went on falling behind my back stop

clouds in the sky motionless as ironed scarves please

recognizing my desire to have things look back at me please

I stare until I consider the scene truly acknowledged stop

a largely gracious gesture but its skin lightly greased for ease of change stop

dry air tonight feathered occasionally with shine stop

I wanted the damp fertile smell even though mold would soon follow stop

a kind of retention that isn't reducible to memory please advise

about the author

Rusty Morrison's first poetry collection, *Whethering*, won the Colorado Prize for Poetry (Center for Literary Publishing 2004), selected by Forrest Gander. She has been a recipient of the Cecil Hemley (2006) and Robert H. Winner (2003) Memorial Awards from The Poetry Society of America, as well as the Society's Alice Fay di Castagnola Award (2007) for a manuscript in progress for *the true keeps calm biding its story*. She has also been a co-winner of the *Five Fingers Review* Poetry Contest (2003). In 2002, she was awarded the Lori and Deke Hunter Fellowship, a residency at the Djerassi Resident Artists Program. One of her poems was selected for the 2005/06 edition of the *Gertrude Stein Awards Anthology*, published by Green Integer Press. She is co-publisher of Omnidawn Publishing.

Ahsahta Press

Ahsahta Press

MODERN AND CONTEMPORARY
POETRY OF THE AMERICAN WEST

Sandra Alcosser, *A Fish to Feed All Hunger*

David Axelrod, *Jerusalem of Grass*

David Baker, *Laws of the Land*

Dick Barnes, *Few and Far Between*

Conger Beasley, Jr., *Over DeSoto's Bones*

Linda Bierds, *Flights of the Harvest-Mare*

Richard Blessing, *Winter Constellations*

Boyer, Burmaster, and Trusky, eds., *The Ahsahta Anthology*

Peggy Pond Church, *New and Selected Poems*

Katharine Coles, *The One Right Touch*

Wyn Cooper, *The Country of Here Below*

Craig Cotter, *Chopstix Numbers*

Judson Crews, *The Clock of Moss*

H. L. Davis, *Selected Poems*

Susan Strayer Deal, *The Dark is a Door*

Susan Strayer Deal, *No Moving Parts*

Linda Dyer, *Fictional Teeth*

Gretel Ehrlich, *To Touch the Water*

Gary Esarey, *How Crows Talk and Willows Walk*

Julie Fay, *Portraits of Women*

Thomas Hornsby Ferril, *Anvil of Roses*

Thomas Hornsby Ferril, *Westering*

Hildegarde Flanner, *The Hearkening Eye*

Charley John Greasybear, *Songs*

Corrinne Hales, *Underground*

Hazel Hall, *Selected Poems*

Nan Hannon, *Sky River*

Gwendolen Haste, *Selected Poems*

Kevin Hearle, *Each Thing We Know Is Changed Because We Know It And Other Poems*

Sonya Hess, *Kingdom of Lost Waters*

Cynthia Hogue, *The Woman in Red*

Robert Krieger, *Headlands, Rising*

Elio Emiliano Ligi, *Disturbances*

Haniel Long, *My Seasons*

Ken McCullough, *Sycamore•Oriole*

Norman MacLeod, *Selected Poems*

Barbara Meyn, *The Abalone Heart*

David Mutschlecner, *Esse*

Dixie Partridge, *Deer in the Haystacks*

Gerrye Payne, *The Year-God*

George Perreault, *Curved Like an Eye*

Howard W. Robertson, *to the fierce guard in the Assyrian Saloon*

Leo Romero, *Agua Negra*

Leo Romero, *Going Home Away Indian*

Miriam Sagan, *The Widow's Coat*

Philip St. Clair, *At the Tent of Heaven*

Philip St. Clair, *Little-Dog-of-Iron*

Donald Schenker, *Up Here*

Gary Short, *Theory of Twilight*

D. J. Smith, *Prayers for the Dead Ventriloquist*

Richard Speakes, *Hannah's Travel*

Genevieve Taggard, *To the Natural World*

Tom Trusky, ed., *Women Poets of the West*

Marnie Walsh, *A Taste of the Knife*

Bill Witherup, *Men at Work*

Carolyne Wright, *Stealing the Children*

This book is set in Apollo MT type with Futura Standard titles
by Ahsahta Press at Boise State University
and manufactured according to the Green Press Initiative
by Thomson-Shore, Inc.
Cover design by Quemadura.
Book design by Janet Holmes.

AHSAHTA PRESS

2007

JANET HOLMES, DIRECTOR

STEFFEN BROWN

NAOMI TARLE

J R WALSH

DENNIS BARTON, INTERN

DALE SPANGLER, INTERN